SO YOU WANT TO BUY

a small business?

BY: JOE VAGNONE

AuthorHouse™
1663 Liberty Drive
Bloomington, IN 47403
www.authorhouse.com
Phone: 1-800-839-8640

First published by AuthorHouse 03/02/2011

ISBN: 978-1-4567-1958-6 (sc)
ISBN: 978-1-4567-1957-9 (dj)
ISBN: 978-1-4567-5453-2 (e)

Library of Congress Control Number: 2011901325

Printed in the United States of America

Any people depicted in stock imagery provided by Thinkstock are models, and such images are being used for illustrative purposes only. Certain stock imagery © Thinkstock.

This book is printed on acid-free paper.

PREFACE

Buying or selling a small business can be overwhelming. You will have many questions, and this book does not have all the answers; however, I hope you will benefit from these pages by discovering which questions you need to ask. By addressing many of these concerns along the way, I hope this book will encourage and inspire you to venture into the world of business ownership.

CONTRIBUTORS

Those that were most helpful toward the completion of this book are listed below.

Dr. Roy Mason

Chelsea "Little Bit" Bren

Leslie Ogle

Thanks, guys.

"There are always opportunities through which businessmen can profit handsomely, if they will only recognize and seize them."

- J. Paul Getty

TABLE OF CONTENTS

"Think
about your
business as
a customer."

Nick
Evgenitakis
Sunrise Restaurant

IT STARTS WITHIN YOU.
your life is about to change!

The idea of a person stepping into the world of small business ownership is exciting.

I can vividly remember, like it was yesterday, when my mom, on her own volition, got a $12,000 second mortgage on her home so that I could buy my first restaurant. Little did I realize the impact that motherly gesture of love and generosity would have on my life. Thanks Mom!

Small business ownership is, in my opinion, the very foundation of the American experience. Liberty and freedom are both the results and causes of capitalism. Without them all working congruently, it would be impossible for our nation and her citizens to survive through the choppy waters of ever-changing economic times.

As you go through these pages, I hope to give you ideas, concepts, and life experiences that you can use to make wise decisions

"thanks mom!"

in your life—decisions that will propel you into a lifestyle that will define and meet your expectations. Along the way, I trust that you will be challenged to hear the voice of God through the scriptural thoughts dispersed throughout this book.

After all, (I try to remember), the greatest need in all of our lives is a personal relationship with the Lord Jesus Christ. This is the only path to true happiness. Also, I hope you will hear wisdom in the quotes from small business people I have had the privilege of meeting over the years.

ONE OF MY GOALS IN WRITING THIS BOOK is to show you that the path to small business ownership is shorter than you ever imagined…and much more fun! But before we get started, I want to try and open your mind to the many possibilities that are right under your nose—all we have to do is be willing to place ourselves in a mind set that will allow us to hear and see these opportunities.

For example: I'm a person that gets excited every day to hear of a new approach to something. My mind is always open to ideas, new concepts and visions. But it was not always that way for me.

I can remember (I still laugh as I think about it) the first day of summer of my junior year of high school. My buddy, Chuck Howell, and I wanted some extra money for dating, gas etc. I came up with this great Nobel Prize winning idea. "Chuck, let's wash cars," I said with excitement…as if no one had ever thought of it. "I can make a flyer that looks good; we can pass it around the neighborhoods, and people will pay us good money."

Like most ideas of mine, Chuck rolled his eyes and said, "Man, that sounds like a lot of work for $10." I quickly barked back, "Come on Chuck, it will be great! I can make a door hanger that people will really respond to."

I could tell from the look in his eyes that I was losing him so I said, "I will pay for the flyers and pass them out…all you have to do is help clean the cars." Chuck's response was funny—as he walked away shaking his head he said, "There has got to be a better way to make money than this, so I'm going to give the idea of making money some more thought."

I'm thinking that while he is looking for the next big idea to make money, I will be making money. The next day, Chuck calls me and says, "Hey man, I got an idea… how about if we just put a $5 ad in the paper and tell people we will haul off their junk?" I wasted no time telling Chuck that it was a stupid idea. "Who in their right mind," I said, "would pay to get rid of the very same stuff they did not want?" But, after all, I'm a person who will try anything so I said, "Ok…but you have to pay the $5 for the ad." Chuck agreed.

So I spent $145 on car wash flyers, and I spent many hours hanging the flyers on doors. We received two calls for car washes…one was my mom's car and the other was my neighbor's. It took us three hours to clean each of those cars—six hours for $20.

The day we finished our second customer's car, the ad ran for the junk hauling business. The ad read, "Have truck, will haul…call Chuck." Yeah, you guessed it! We stayed busy all summer hauling junk and made well over $20 an hour. Chuck never said a word comparing the two ideas; he just kept calling with more jobs. I still, to this day, will never forget Chuck's "Nobel Prize" idea.

Seek first the Kingdom of God and His righteousness and

all these things will be added

unto you.

- Matthew 6:33

LET OTHERS SEE WHAT JESUS LOOKS LIKE DOING YOUR JOB.
- *Dr. Roy Mason*

joe's T O P reasons

TO BUY A BUSINESS

There is a plethora of reasons for buying a business, but I think a concise list would include:

QUALITY OF LIFESTYLE: While being a small business owner does not mean that every day will be spent playing golf or fishing, it does mean that you could spend your days doing the things you enjoy. Think about it; if you are doing the things you have a passion for, won't your life be more fulfilling? And a fulfilled life is a better life!

HUGE TAX BENEFITS: Now I'm not an accountant so I will not attempt to give financial advice here, but there are many legal avenues afforded to the small business which will help defer and reduce your tax liabilities. This benefit works well in coordination with your current job if your small business is a secondary source of income. We'll talk more about this later in the book.

A PEACE OF MIND: Although none of us are in control of our lives (God is ultimately in control), the small business model gives you far more control than simply working for someone else. Small business ownership, when coupled with your spouse's income or a "company job," grants you much additional security and flexibility. Essentially you will not be putting all your eggs in one basket.

YOU GET TO GIVE BACK: You contribute to your town, city and the world in ways that make a real difference in the lives of people you may never know otherwise. I like to think of it in a very simple way. Giving enables you to fill the world with possibilities and pleasures where you think it's needed. In many cases, it is not just through money. Rather it's through action and living your life in transparency so others see God in your daily life.

Now I know what you are thinking, "WOW! Making money is not one of the top reasons for owning a small business?" That's right. Most small business operations within the first three years do not make the owner enough money to satisfy their expectations.

Now is a great time to ask yourself:
- *Why do you want to be in business for yourself?*
- *What is your expectation for personal income?*

If you cannot answer these two questions with honesty and clarity do not read any further. If you cannot position your life according to the answers you give to the questions above, then go out today and get a job working for someone else.

You must have the frame of mind that says, "I will do whatever it takes to make this new business work!" If you do not go into the venture with this attitude, you're not ready to be self-employed. And you would serve your-self and your family well to go get a JOB!

Remember, being self-employed is a life full of unknowns. If you do not have a measure of self-confidence and determination, there is no way you can teach and inspire others to come work alongside you. But if you have this self confidence, read on because I can help you get what you want. I will not have all the answers, but I will have ideas, plans, and visions which will allow you to fill in the blanks with your hard work, skills, and dreams.

"WOW! Making money is not one of the top reasons for owning a small business?"

"Don't fall in love with the latest hot concept to appear on the horizon if it is not a good fit for you."

Randy Mitchell

esource USA

CHAPTER TWO

O W N
your next job

The question is what do you do if you find your-self without a job or if your current position is in jeopardy? The idea of just simply finding another job may not be that easy anymore. The reality of making 25 to 35 percent less in salary, and having a schedule that is not flexible or family-friendly, is a real possibility.

There are many small businesses for sale and opportunities for good profit margins. Most of these businesses need an owner with certain skill sets. In some cases, the present owners cannot make it through tough financial times because they may lack the business knowledge or skill set necessary to maintain the business in a challenging market. In other cases, the present owners are ready to retire, and the "financial" timing is right. Whatever the reason, there are many opportunities that can put you back in the workforce—working for yourself!

For most people, it boils down to the question of money. The truth is that there are many businesses for sale where the owner will finance. When working through the financing of a small business, there are numerous options, many of which would not require a bank. If you want to own your own business, rest assured that there are many ways to make it happen.

Most people are unaware that a 401-k account can be used to start a new business without any penalty or tax. In a climate of uncertainty, people should not hesitate to trust their money to work for them. One example is using the business cash flow to help with the down payment; the terms and deals are endless. You will find it amazing how easy it can be to be in business for yourself.

In fact, the time invested to find and buy a business of your own could be much shorter than finding a new job. Another thing to consider is a business that is operating well on its own. Just giving the business a few hours a day or week could help make up the difference in a salary loss. There are many franchises and independent businesses that can provide a great secondary income.

You may wonder why you would want to invest your money in a business when so many small businesses are in trouble. The secret to buying a small business is to buy right. The economy will have trends but, if you buy right, downward trends will not devastate your business.

Perhaps you have been advised not to "buy" yourself a job, but I truly believe it just might be the answer for many people—with little risk compared to the riskiness of the stock market these past years. It is time you trust in yourself and your skills and take the helm by owning your job, instead of letting someone else control your destiny!

what business is ?
RIGHT FOR YOU

W hat gets you excited when you wake up in the morning? What is it that you look forward to on a professional level? For me, I really enjoy the prospect of helping people find the right business and putting the deal together.

I'm not saying that simply because you love cake, you should look to buy a bakery, nor am I saying that because you like to look through car magazines, you should buy a car lot. What I am saying is this: The skill sets you already possess (and the life and professional experiences you have) will likely translate very well into other industries that utilize the same skills.

"It's imperative that you understand my definitions of 'Entrepreneur' and 'Small Business Owner.'"

An excellent way to find the right opportunity is to look at enough businesses until you find a place where your skill sets and interests intersect.

Before I go any further, it is imperative that you understand my definitions of "entrepreneur" and "small business owner." The entrepreneur is first and foremost a self-confident, risk-taking, visionary who translates the vision into action. The small business owner is the person who enjoys the day-to-day details of the enterprise and is often an excellent manager. To better illustrate this point, I would say that an entrepreneur looks for a reason to buy while a small business owner looks for reasons not to buy, even though both might eventually reach the same conclusion.

It has been my experience that the entrepreneur has more than one business…not because he needs to but rather it's because he gets bored and needs another challenge. At the same time, a small business person sees no value or rationale in multiple operations or businesses until the business fully demands and requires the action.

In my case, I had many restaurants inside office buildings and manufacturing plants. I found myself spending much more time working on the next location than on the business of operating a restaurant company. I found myself looking forward to the negotiations of a new lease much more than the process of implementing new menu ideas or hiring employees. You guessed it! I'm an entrepreneur.

I would compare an entrepreneur and a small business owner to a pastor and an evangelist. The pastor needs and uses the various ministries of a local church to share Christ with people while the evangelist shares the Gospel with anyone who will listen. The pastor enjoys the managerial duties of the entire church, while the evangelist is more singularly focused on his broad vision of reaching the world for Christ. In this comparison, I would paint the pastor as a small business owner and the evangelist as the entrepreneur.

I'm not suggesting one is better than the other. Entrepreneurs often have a more difficult time making money than the small business person does. Remember, entrepreneurs are visionaries – calculated risk-takers driven by an idea. Small business owners often are rewarded as a successful manager and operator in a specific business that meets all their expectations.

The question is, "Which one are you?" The answer will help you know which business to buy.

"…Look at enough businesses until you find a place where your skill sets and interests intersect.

25

For to me, to live is Christ and to die is gain.

- Philippians 1:22

LET OTHERS SEE WHAT JESUS LOOKS LIKE DOING YOUR JOB.
- *Dr. Roy Mason*

seller?
FINANCING

I have seller-financed nearly every business I have ever bought or sold. To date, I have been involved in more than 75 of these business ventures. I must admit that I love seller financing.

Perhaps you are asking, "What is seller financing?"

As part of the negotiations, the potential buyer will ask for or the seller will offer financing. This makes the conventional process of going to a commercial lender unnecessary since the seller will be the lender, requiring a non-refundable deposit and creating a payment plan for the balance due on the business. There will likely be no additional collateral required of the buyer since the actual business will be the security for the financing.

HERE IS A LIST OF SOME OF THE REASONS I FAVOR USING THIS METHOD OF FINANCING:

• The seller can ask for a higher price (in some cases as much as 25% higher) since he/she is assuming some risk but is confident in the buyer's ability to operate the business successfully. This should also increase the comfort level for the buyer.

• The seller will continue to profit from interest on the financed portion of the loan, which provides more income than that of a straight cash sale.

• The length of time to close an owner-financed business agreement will be substantially less than that of a conventional, commercial lender, which is often laborious, painful, and impersonal.

• The buyer can be confident the seller feels good about the future of the business because he/she continues to have a vested interest in the success of both the business and the buyer.

• The seller will be more likely to advise and answer the buyer's questions (at least through the financing period) to ensure the success of the business and its operation.

• The deal gets done much easier because both parties can be very creative with the terms, payments, pay-off dates, etc.

• This type of financing goes a long way in building a long-term relationship between the buyer and the seller which will be based on honesty, integrity, and common interests.

It is important to remember that while there are a few limited risks involved in the seller-financing model, these are substantially outweighed by the positives listed here. Furthermore, the creative seller-financing model makes it much easier to sell your business. Remember, nearly 90% of all small business sales utilize this method.

"Run a tight profit and loss (P&L) and cater to your clients."

— Rick Ruby

The Core Training, Inc

For where your treasure is, there your heart will be also.

- Matthew 6:21

LET OTHERS SEE WHAT JESUS LOOKS LIKE DOING YOUR JOB.
- Dr. Roy Mason

CHAPTER FIVE

DO I HAVE ENOUGH MONEY
to buy a business?

S omeone once asked John D. Rockefeller, the industrial tycoon, "How much money is enough?" He simply responded, "Just a little bit more." That is a good way to think about starting comfortably in a business. If you do not have Rockefeller cash, there are some things you can look at to determine if your resources will be enough.

• First you need to create a cash flow projection that includes new expenses for the business based on your future plans. It is very important that you use all the line item expenses in the seller's chart of accounts in your projections. This conservative approach will serve you well as you are leaving nothing out that may surprise you later. There was a reason the seller had that line item, so it is best to include the expense even if it is a small amount. Also, do not forget your estimated payment for the purchase of the business.

This exercise will give you a starting point for how much cash you will need when thinking about your improvements and changes as well as your marketing and promotional vision for the company. If this cash flow calculation produces a negative number, it is best to multiply that by six months at least. Again, taking a conservative approach allows you the time to turn your business into a profitable venture while limiting what otherwise would be the unexpected expenses. The cash requirement must also include the initial down payment; therefore serious inquiry needs to be made concerning this figure.

• Next you will need to price out in great detail all the changes you would like to make in the business. The goal of all of these changes should be geared directly to create profit as soon as possible. Make sure you start this process before you buy or even finalize an offer to buy. You need to know how much your vision of the future will cost. You cannot guess these figures and costs effectively. You have to know these costs concretely. After you buy the business, it is simply too late to find out that your new plans, as grand and spectacular as they are, will not be cost effective.

• The other aspect to consider is your level of willingness to sacrifice for the health and survival of the business. Determine how long you are willing to put any profit back into the company to help with the start-up costs. Determine where your cash is coming from and make sure you account for the cost of that money. Living expenses and the cost of taking money out of savings are examples that should be included in your cash requirement projections as well.

Furthermore, you must account for professional fees from an attorney and CPA as well as fees associated with paperwork at the closing. Available working capital should be from five to ten percent of the total cash requirement figure that is produced at the end of this planning exercise.

Do not let all of these costs scare you! Keep your eye on relishing the opportunity to become a business owner. The bottom line to this approach is that you cannot overstate costs and expenses as part of your due diligence when considering the purchase of a business. In reality, these numbers will be much smaller, or nonexistent, as your firm footing in the operation takes over. The alternative to this approach can be rife with unwelcome surprises or even regrets.

With a note of encouragement, I can tell you with confidence and experience that opportunities do exist, and some are right under your nose. Be acutely aware of your surroundings and be on the lookout for business deals that get you excited!

"Do not let all of these costs scare you! Keep your eye on relishing the opportunity to become a business owner."

"Know exactly the cost of doing business. Slow down and do your homework, do not get caught up in the excitement and make the wrong move."

Alan Schmidt

Greenway Lawn Management

the perfect
DEAL

The process of buying my first new car took five months to complete. First came the hours spent driving up and down car lots just looking at the stickers on the windows. Then I started to walk into the dealership showrooms and offices but would not talk to any of the salesmen, pushy as they all were. By the second month of these preliminary exercises, the realization that I would have to talk to them in order to buy a new car became painfully apparent.

The car that I wanted was a Ford Escort, and I had extensive notes on that model of car, the dealerships offering that car, as well as consumer reports reviewing it. I was fully loaded with information. However, what I lacked was the ability to make a decision about spending my money, fearing I would pay too much. I was stymied! But I pressed on.

The Ford dealer that I had been to three times prior was again blessed with my presence. When I pulled up, it was snowing and there were no other customers in sight. With notes in hand, I walked in. The usual fanfare, scurrying salesmen ready to pounce, and offers of a drink or cookies were conspicuously absent. There was one very large man, at least six feet tall, sitting in a chair laughing, obviously amused.

"Big man," he bellowed. "Come on over here."

As he was still laughing, I pointed to myself and looked around and asked, "Me?"

"Yeah big man, come here," he said again, still chuckling away.

After inquiring as to what was tickling him so much he said, "You are, big man, you are cracking me up! We had a bet on when the next time would be that you'd show up with your notes. There ain't a salesman in here that thinks you're gonna buy a car, so they all went to the back when they saw you coming!"

"Then why are you still here up front, you draw the short straw?" I asked, trying to turn the embarrassment around.

"No, man, I told them you were driving outta here with a new car!" he said matter-of-factly.

As I stepped closer he said, "Come sit down and get yourself a drink. You know where they are by now. What do you wanna pay for that shiny black Escort that you want so bad? I've seen you more times than my momma the last two months! Before you answer, go out and look at it one more time, look through all them notes, and come back with a price 'cause today you are buying a car!"

"Okay," I said. After twenty minutes, I came back inside.

"You got a once in a lifetime chance to tell me the price you wanna pay. Be fair now!" he said, greeting me on my return.

"I do not know how to answer you," I told him. I knew the other dealers' prices and they were all within $1000 of each other, and here was a guy that was being straight-up honest with me. But I was still frozen with the fear of my figure being accepted. So I said, "I am not sure what a fair price is."

"The best price," he said, "was the price that makes you comfortable, and if you cannot answer that then you will always feel like someone has taken advantage of you. What is the price that makes you feel good about your new car?" he asked again.

After taking a deep breath I said, "I just don't know!" With this I added to my fears that now he would become flustered with me. In fact, I thought he might explode!

Instead, he calmly said, "Okay then, go look at the car again and look at your notes again and then give me a price." I told him it would not help because I know the car and my notes intimately. I just could not commence the negotiations, and I did not know why.

"Then you have wasted your time and that of all the dealers, too," he responded seriously but softly. "Why take all those notes and do all that research if your goal is not finding the right car at the right price? Without that value as a measuring point and without you setting your expectations, you will never get a deal that you're happy with because you don't know what happy is! You need to find it." Then he graciously added, "Man, I'm not selling you a car. I'm giving you a life lesson."

He was, of course, exactly right. I did indeed drive out of that dealership with my brand new car. More importantly, however, I was now in possession of something more profound. Namely, that you cannot enter a transaction without being completely comfortable with the price. In other words, my lesson that day was one of the simplest equations:

THE BEST PRICE OR VALUE = WHAT MAKES YOU COMFORTABLE

Do you grasp the simplicity of this axiom? Your entire purpose should be to feel good about what you have done. All of the exercises that you go through when buying a business should meet this single criterion: there is no right price except the one you determine!

There have been times when I paid too much (for the sake of my argument) for a business according to the raw numbers. But these deals made me comfortable because I knew what could be done and how the venture could grow beyond my expectations. These deals have also proven priceless for the experience I gained as well as the industry contacts I made which have furthered my career in business.

This naturally leads to another principle: It is okay to buy a business based on potential. This may seem a bit too nebulous for the "just the facts ma'am" kind of person, but those cold, analytical types often miss the best opportunities. You do need to fully understand the industry you are considering before this form of value should be used.

For example, I would not think I could pay for potential and get real value if I was buying a pet-grooming business. I know nothing about the business. What would make me think I could do better than the other operators in the industry? Conversely, if you know how to care for animals and enjoy all that goes with the business, then you would consider paying for potential. After all, in my opinion, most of us buy all our investments with an eye toward potential. It may be that the location is very close to your home with only a five-minute commute. That would afford you two hours more a day at the business than the shop for sale across town that has its value based solely on profit and loss statements and balance sheets. Furthermore, it's easier to plug yourself into the community for networking purposes if your business is close to your home. These circumstances are great criteria for evaluating the potential in a business.

What I hope you are seeing is that price and value have more determinants than the black and white figures of a financial statement. The good deal is about all the circumstances, variables, and aspects that enter into the potential equation. There have been several businesses that produced good income for me; I simply did not enjoy them. I had no desire to make that business better. I was ready to sell that business for much less money and I did! If I liked the operation and was willing to stay around until I got a higher price, that would be a different situation. Does that mean I got ripped off? No, it was a case in which I simply took the money and my time and moved on. Everyone was happy and that is the point.

> "The good deal is about all the circumstances, variables, and aspects that enter into the potential equation."

"If you think it will take **10** calls to close a deal, count on **100**."

Dana
Jordan

Lake Norman Woman Magazine, LLC

ten mistakes
TO AVOID

For the past 28 years, I have characterized myself as a "self-employed, small businessman." One thing I know for certain is that I have made numerous mistakes. I have erred far more often than I have succeeded. Perhaps you can learn from some of my mistakes. Here are ten things you should consider (prioritize for yourself) …

• Do not choose a greedy partner. Find a partner who has the success of the business as their priority.

• Do not start too early in life. Learn the basics of the industry while working for someone else. Experiences are expensive; let someone else train you and learn from them.

41

• Do not think that your business will last forever. Most small businesses are a means to an end. You must always be aware of the value of your business in relation to the investments which are placed into it. The investments must never surpass the value of the business.

• Do not think hiring people who know more than you is a good thing. This simply means you do not know enough about your industry. While it is good to employ people with stronger skill sets, you must know your industry.

• Do not under value your employees. Pay them more than you think they are worth, and never treat them as pieces of equipment.

• Do not ignore your competition. Be sure you shop in their stores and buy their products, as much as reasonably possible. You must always be aware of them because they are certainly aware of you.

• Do not fail to market and promote your business. The question is not "should you market" but rather how and where to spend your time and money. Never assume you have the answers. The competition is always watching and will force a change, so always be exploring new ideas on marketing.

• Do not think you will have all the information before you make a decision. You will often be forced to move forward in small business with limited information. You cannot wait for all the options before you act. Sometimes acquiring the information is more challenging, costly and time consuming than the action itself.

• Do not confuse success with wealth. You must understand that being a small business owner is more about your lifestyle choice than a wealth choice. Your decision to move into the realm of small business will give you a lifestyle that is far more liberating than simply working for a company.

42

• Do not forget God. Through the years, nearly all of my poor choices were made apart from God. I am learning more about trusting Him every day, and I welcome you into this journey with me. As my dear friend Dr. Roy Mason (www.gemonline.org) says, "Christ can do more in fifteen minutes than I can do in twenty-four hours." Jesus simply said, "Seek first the kingdom of God and all these things will be added unto you." This certainly includes your small business decisions.

Now is a good time to talk about failing. I have said many times that I like doing business with people who have failed at something before we work together. Not achieving your expectations is hard on families and hard on your ego. Your lifestyle will have to change for a while until you can get back on your feet.

I like telling the story of a client of mine, Atit, who bought a franchise from me years ago and did it with big plans and vision. It was a downtown location with over 5,000 square feet of space, first class all the way. There was nothing like it in the area, short of a small food court.

After many months of hard work and a lot of money, he came to the realization that the idea was not going to work. We can talk about why the business failed, but that would fill a book all in itself. So we will leave that to another time. The reason I bring this up is because I have never witnessed a person who had lost so much and yet his character and approach to getting out of business was as impressive as his entry into business. I have immense respect for him. I have told him that I hope my son, when he grows up, would have half the character I witnessed in him as he went through what had to be one of the hardest times in his life.

Today he and his wife still own one of the restaurants that I sold to them, and it is doing very well. There is life after a failed business. Your character is defined by how you handle the tough times. Atit, my friend, you have my respect. Job well done! You are an inspiration to many who know your story.

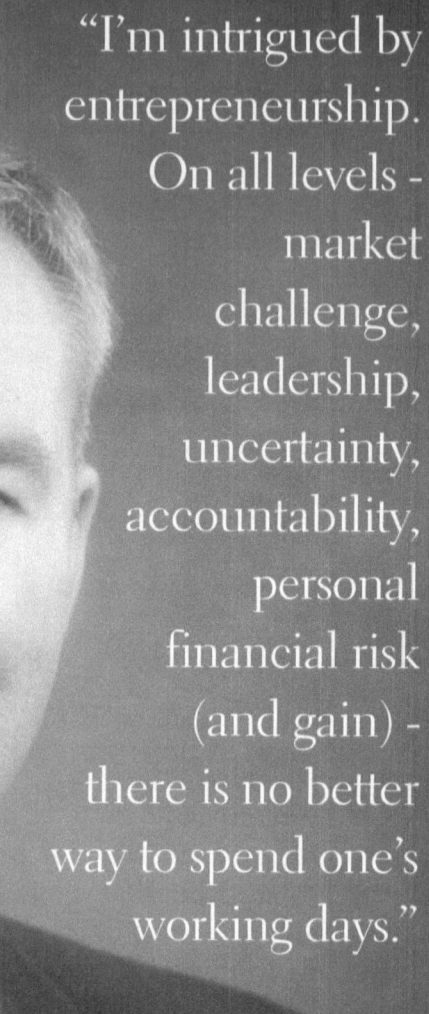

"I'm intrigued by entrepreneurship. On all levels - market challenge, leadership, uncertainty, accountability, personal financial risk (and gain) - there is no better way to spend one's working days."

Dave
Gilroy

Scale Finance LLC

CHAPTER EIGHT

BUYING A BUSINESS:

too risky or a sound investment?

To answer such a broad question requires a closer look at the investor rather than at the investment. Most of the time, of course, it is simply hard work that yields the most success in small business. That is the general answer to the question. If you apply great effort in a way that is honorable and sound, you can be rewarded for your investment of time and money. But getting at the heart of the matter is neither easy nor simple because everyone has their own set of issues and circumstances as a potential investor or buyer.

There are several aspects to consider when determining if buying a small business is a prudent action or not. For example, if it is your goal to have your money do all the work for you, buying a small business may not be the right thing for you.

45

Stocks, bonds, and certainly real estate, are great wealth-building tools. But, in most cases, these ventures are out of your direct control once the initial decisions to invest are made. By contrast, with small business, your money simply buys you the opportunity and then it is up to you to "work" that business to success.

This simplistic comparison serves only to define interests and skills. In no way am I suggesting that a person can only do one or the other. In fact, I would recommend both. I have made as much money in real estate as I have in any small business I have owned and operated. Remember, you are investing in yourself! You want that part of the equation working as hard as it can. Therefore, you must be willing to expend time and energy; otherwise you should invest in the company of the guy who does work hard in his business!

Knowing what investment level you are comfortable with and having a realistic expectation of the return on your money and time will also help you realize what type of business is right for you. The right timing often plays an important part. For example, you may have all your ducks in a row, ready to buy a business, but the opportunities are not available at a price or in terms you are comfortable with. Conversely, the opportunity may be there but you are not ready personally or financially to take advantage, hence, the timing is not right. These risk factors enter the equation more often than not. The true entrepreneur or small business person will find a way to manage the risks, work through them, and venture into his desired business. Accordingly, you must work more diligently than others do even before you write the first check.

Putting these components together eases your transition into business. At the right time, with realistic expectations of slow growth, you can turn a struggling small business into a profitable enterprise. You may find the deal of a lifetime. You may find the type of deal that you've read about in success stories. Many times, the key is to act when others are afraid to make a move. Risk is to be avoided if possible but, in reality, calculated and mitigated risk is what small business is all about.

"...Calculated and mitigated risk is what small business is all about."

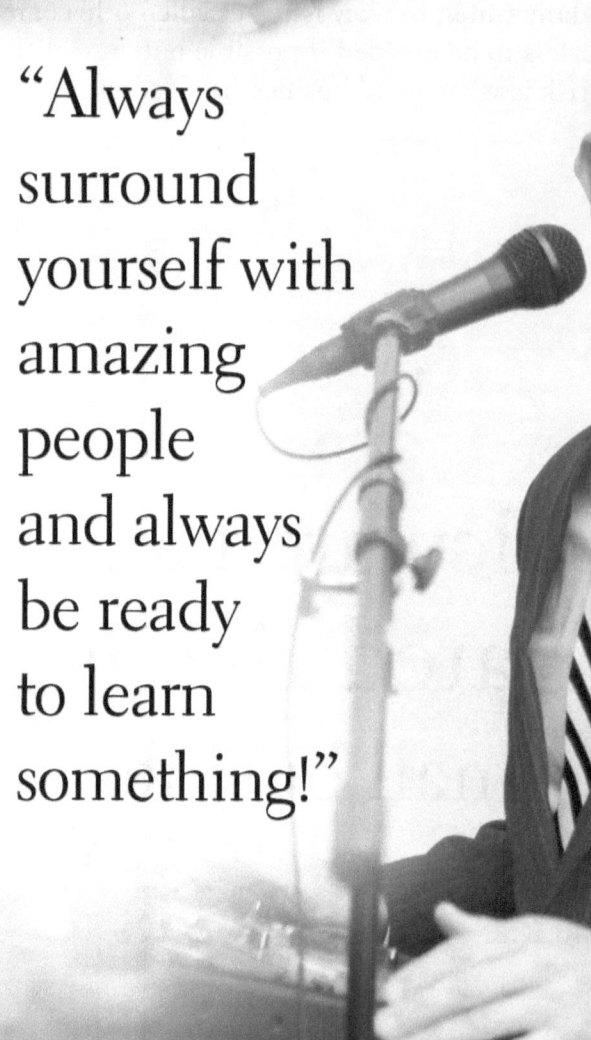

"Always surround yourself with amazing people and always be ready to learn something!"

Michael
Catlow
The Michael Catlow Group

hiring
PROFESSIONALS

This is a process that will take you some time. I'm astonished at the people who walk into my office and ask me, at the last minute, "Do you know an attorney to help me look at the closing documents?"

You will need an experienced transactional or small business attorney long before you actually buy the business. You should interview at least three attorneys, three accountants, and two insurance agents before you make an offer on anything. This will help you get an understanding of what they believe is necessary as due-diligence on the buying of your business. You must always be completely honest and forthright with these professionals. In other words, don't tell these professionals that you are contemplating buying three coffee shops when you are actually only looking to buy one. Be completely honest!

This interviewing process will afford you the advantage of building lasting relationships with the appropriate professionals. Remember, they will be working for you, so a healthy relationship is vital. Here are some questions to consider asking:

- DO YOU HELP CLIENTS BUY AND SELL BUSINESSES?

- HOW MANY IN THE LAST YEAR?

- DO YOU WORK ON FRANCHISEES ACQUISITIONS?

- WHAT ARE YOUR RATES?

- HOW OPEN IS YOUR SCHEDULE?

- CAN YOU RECOMMEND AN ACCOUNTANT/ ATTORNEY/ INSURANCE AGENCY?

- ARE YOU COMFORTABLE GIVING ME A FEW REFERENCES OF THOSE YOU HAVE HELPED WITH RECENT ACQUISITIONS?

- HOW QUICKLY SHOULD I EXPECT TO GET ANSWERS FROM YOU?

- HOW EARLY DO YOU ARRIVE IN THE MORNING?

- HOW LATE DO YOU STAY IN THE EVENING?

- HOW MUCH OF A NOTICE WILL YOU REQUIRE TO EMPLOY YOUR SERVICES?

Please remember. Do not let these professionals become the negotiators of your deal. I cannot tell you how many lawyers and accountants think they are good negotiators and businesspersons when in fact they are not. If you hear nothing else from this chapter, hear this—you alone should determine the amount of risk you are willing to take. Let the professionals help you define and understand the risk, but the risk and choice is yours.

do I need
A BROKER?

Buying a business is much different than any other real estate transaction. Because businesses do not simply place a "for sale" sign in their window, you will need the services of a good business broker to help you identify and locate potential business opportunities for your consideration.

My experiences with business brokers are within North and South Carolina where there is no formal Multiple Listing Service for businesses (MLS) like you would be accustomed to in real estate. This online service allows all real estate brokers and agents to share information on all listings so that any agent can sell any property.

Because there are no services available for businesses, your job to find a small business is much harder and more time consuming. Unless the broker you visit will co-broker, they can only show you the businesses they have listed. That means you will need to go to many brokers to look at many businesses for sale because, without co-brokering, there is no compensation for their efforts.

I have a great deal of respect for good brokers. Their biggest job is to get the personalities of the buyers and sellers out of the way of a deal. If you think this is an easy task, you are in for a rough road when buying a business because it is all about emotion. Buyers are paranoid that the seller is taking advantage of them. Sellers are frightened that their life's work is not being properly valued, and may be concerned that no one will ever be able to run the business as well as they did.

Also, the detailed, formal process of making an offer requires many contingencies which can be intimidating to both the buyer and seller. The third-party (broker) will help interpret the contingencies which will be helpful to both of the parties involved.

Since 1980, I have bought or owned no fewer than 75 separate businesses. Many of them I bought without using a broker, but discovered that my most successful deals always involved the services of a business broker. I learned, and still believe, that the more inexperienced the buyer or seller, the more you want a broker helping the deal come together.

In many cases, it takes the broker to list and confirm the buyer's qualifications in making the seller feel comfortable with the owner-financing portion of the deal. It takes the broker to gather and evaluate a buyer's financial position before recommending the owner-finance proposal to the seller. These are much more difficult to accomplish without a broker in the process representing both parties in the discussion. There is always a delicate balancing of information, privacy, and confidentiality for both parties.

The value of a broker is not in finding you a business to buy, but rather it is in making the entire deal work.

There is a need for trust and respect from both sides of a good deal. Very few deals ever get done if the process is adversarial. A good broker takes the wishes and needs of both parties and helps form a level of trust and respect for each other. It has been my experience that this most often happens when the buyer, seller, and broker work cooperatively toward a common goal. The specific interests of the three may be different, but the goal is the same – closing the deal. If you do not trust and respect your broker, you should look for another.

"The value of a broker is not in finding you a business to buy, but rather it is in making the entire deal work."

QUALIFICATIONS OF A BROKER:

There are no formal qualifications for business brokers, although some states require the broker to have a real estate license. Here is a list of questions to ask a broker before you decide on one:

(*Note: Remember to always research the broker on the Internet.)

- HAVE YOU OWNED YOUR OWN BUSINESS?

- WHAT WERE THE GROSS SALES OF THE BUSINESS YOU OWNED?

- DID YOU SELL IT? IF SO, DID YOU USE A BROKER?

- HOW MANY LISTINGS DO YOU CURRENTLY HAVE?

- HOW DO YOU DETERMINE WHAT LISTINGS TO TAKE?

- HOW WOULD YOU DESCRIBE YOUR NEGOTIATING SKILLS?

- MAY I SEE A COPY OF THE AGREEMENT YOU WOULD LIKE FOR ME TO SIGN IF I MAKE AN OFFER?

- WHAT ARE YOUR SPECIALTY INDUSTRIES?

- WHAT ARE YOUR GREATEST STRENGTHS?

- WHAT ARE YOUR GREATEST WEAKNESSES?

- WHAT IS EXPECTED OF ME?

- MAY I HAVE TWO REFERENCES?

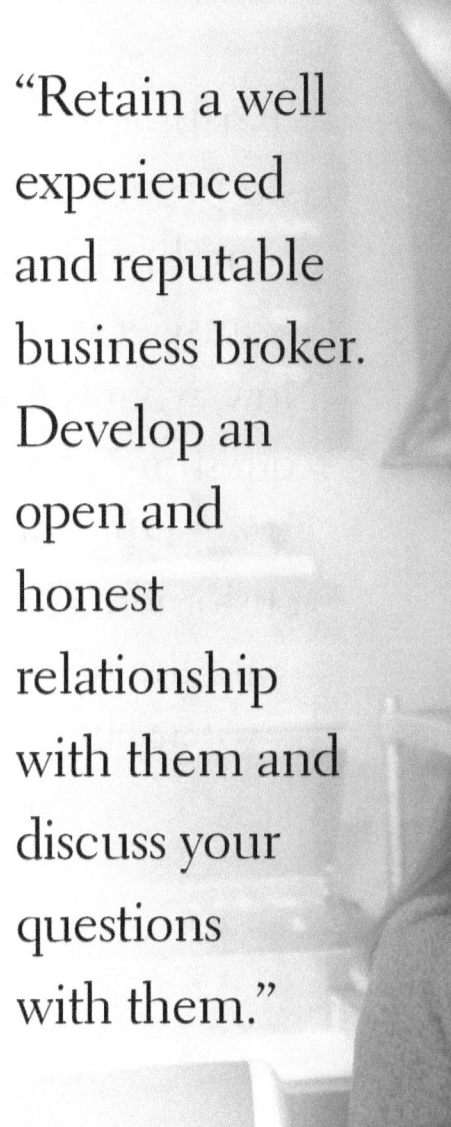

"Retain a well experienced and reputable business broker. Develop an open and honest relationship with them and discuss your questions with them."

Mina
Mashruwala

Midday at The Tower

"Embrace two basic precepts of doing business: 'The answer is yes. Now, what is the question?' And: 'Hug your customer. They are the reason we are here.'"

Donna
Neely

Centurion Development
& Entrepreneur

valuing a small
BUSINESS

There are several ways to value a small business. I have utilized most of them when helping clients.

The first topic I want to address is the question, "How do I put a price tag on goodwill, great brand recognition, synergy options, and upward industry trends?"

Many will advise you to avoid a pricing method which includes these "intangibles" because they believe the value is always in line with current performance and present cash flow. The truth is, however, I have never met a seller that doesn't expect these intangibles to be included in the price. Unless their personal circumstances force the sale, they will just keep the business until they die or give it to their kids. Your task, as a buyer, is to work through the emotions of the seller and arrive at a fair price that works within your goals, limitations, and expectations.

This reminds me of a closet manufacturing business that I bought a few years ago and I paid over $100k more than what the cash-flow and assets of the business would support. I arrived at this number because I believed that I could increase sales by at least $1 million by simply applying the industry multiple to the potential future sales which would easily justify my offer to purchase.

It is reasonable to pay what might otherwise seem like an inflated cost for a business as long as the terms support the offer. Let me reiterate, TERMS ARE AS IMPORTANT AS PRICE. In the case of this closet manufacturing business, the seller received payment in the form of "percentage of sales." In my mind, the business paid for the business which required no capital from me and allowed me to support the final sales price because I was buying potential.

The traditional methods I'm sharing with you are very helpful tools, but they are not an exact science. Professionals, like attorneys and accountants, often have a difficult time trying to value a small business because they are most likely trained to look exclusively at hard evidence rather than the big potential picture. Because there are so many moving parts, very few businesses are exactly alike. Even a franchise that should, in theory, be identical to the one down the street, might have things like location, tenant mix, rental rate, personnel, future required up-fit costs, and competition that will dramatically alter the price.

HERE ARE SOME TRADITIONAL METHODS USED FOR VALUING A SMALL BUSINESS:

• ASSET-BASED VALUATIONS

In small business, the assets are things like furniture, fixtures, equipment, and inventory. In most cases, this method has very little to do with the value of the business. I believe the buyer needs to see these assets simply as tools of the real value which should help them create "cash flow."

• MULTIPLE OF CASH FLOW METHOD

This is one form of valuation that has to be considered with any offer to purchase. The real cash flow, or adjusted cash flow, is calculated starting with the profit & loss statement; adding back any expenses that you would get some benefit from if you were the owner. You can do this using tax returns as well. I have listed some of these add backs below:

Car payments, car insurance, including that of spouses and children
Health insurance, life insurance, spouses and children's as well
401K, IRA
Charitable contributions
Country club dues
Travel, meals and entertainment
Non-working family members
Personal utilities
One-time expenses like big repairs or purchases

• MULTIPLE OF SALES METHOD

I use this for a baseline, but it is not my favorite valuation because with so many factors, just using sales overlooks too many variables.

Example: Let's take a "franchise sandwich shop" whose multiple is almost 70% of sales.

First shop: has $400,000 in sales with a cash flow of $60,000 per year. That's 18% profit (sale price would be 70% of $400,000 or $280,000)

Second shop: has $370,000 in sales with a cash flow of $81,000 per year. That's a 22% profit (sale price would be 70% of $370,000 or $259,000)

The difference in the second shop is in the payroll, rent and the fact that it is in a small town with lower costs and no competition, so they can charge more for a drink or chips. These are real and need to be accounted for in the sales price.

● RETURN ON INVESTMENT

Of all the methods, this is my favorite because I can factor in the terms of the deal and, based on my beliefs in the future of the business, I am able to decide exactly what return, on my cash, makes me comfortable. I know there are some egg heads that say you need to factor the return on the total sales price of the business. I do look at that as a baseline but in general and within reason, if I'm not writing a check for it and the business is paying for the business, then why do I need to put a lot of weight on the total return of a sale price when I've only put down 10%? In my view, for small businesses, there are three returns I look at: my money, my time, and my risk. I will then compare this return to the other investment options I have available to me at that time.

● RULE OF THUMB METHOD

This is the gathering of data on the particular industry, into which you are buying, which gives you basic and general information on sales, expenses, and costs involved with valuing the particular business. Without this market-driven data, which includes sales calculations and the like, a potential buyer is just guessing as to what the honest value of a business might be. In our firm, we use several rules of thumb and create an average which gives us a great starting point for a seller and a clear understanding from the buyer how the seller came to a price.

● REPLACEMENT COST

This method is simply asking the question, "If I had to start from scratch, how much would it cost to duplicate this exact business?"

If it's a franchise, the answer is quite simple. Most franchises (FDD or UFOC) have that information clearly stated and, in most cases, on their websites. If it is an independent operation, this could be a complicated answer. Make sure you calculate time and money before the new operation is in a cash-flowing position. I have a quick rule for this: If the business has been operating successfully in the same location for more than five years, chances are you will spend a lot more cash attempting to duplicate that business.

For additional reading on these methods, I suggest that you study Richard Parker's training course, "How to Buy A Good Business At A Great Price" (Diomo Corporation) which will prove to be worthy of your time and money.

"Your task, as a buyer, is to work through the emotions of the seller and arrive at a fair price that works within your goals, limitations, and expectations."

61

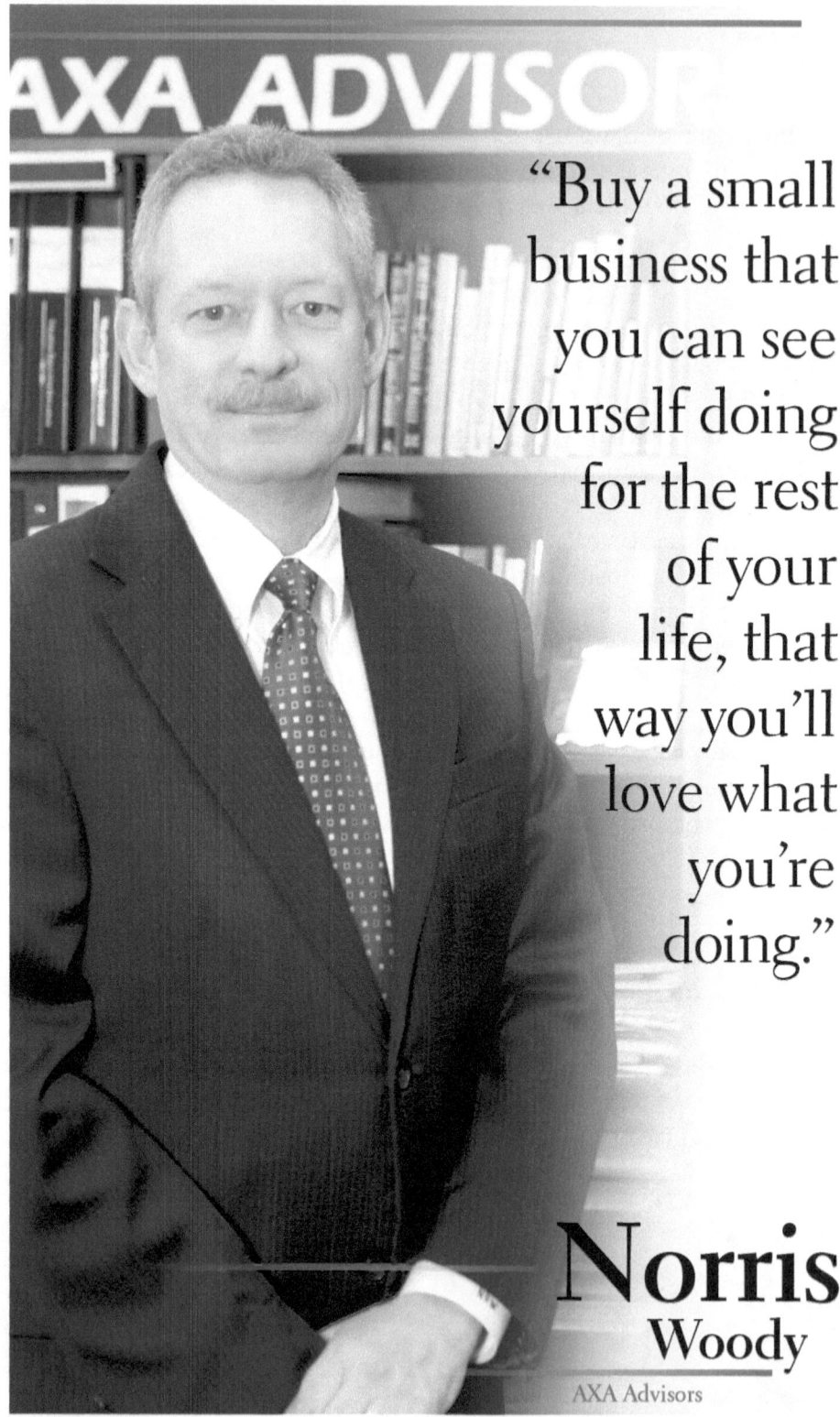

AXA ADVISO

"Buy a small business that you can see yourself doing for the rest of your life, that way you'll love what you're doing."

Norris
Woody

AXA Advisors

CHAPTER TWELVE

NEGOTIATING

The most complicated and difficult area in the small business process is certainly negotiations. Negotiations will involve emotions, feelings, expectations, and questions from the parties on both sides of the table. Think about the last time you haggled with a car dealer for a new car. Whatever emotional struggles you encountered while sitting across the desk from that salesman will be multiplied immeasurably when you begin to negotiate for your new business.

You must never forget that negotiations always involve multiple parties. The person sitting across the table from you has just as much at stake as do you. As the buyer, you are looking for the opportunity to enter into a new chapter of your life, while the seller is about to close a very important chapter of his/her life. Most likely, the seller spent years developing his or her business—a business that has provided for a home, the raising of children…allowing a certain kind of lifestyle. Your attempt to know the other party is just as important as knowing the business that you are buying. Because of this, I have often paid more for businesses than I originally thought they were worth. You must always be willing to pay more than you think you should.

"Why would I be willing to do this?" you might ask. I can answer that with one word: TERMS! Good terms that allow the business to pay for the business will make most of the difference between the buyer's offer and the seller's price. This will only occur when both parties have an honest understanding of each other.

It would be a mistake for me to lead you to believe that the negotiating process is always smooth and painless. Often, even when both parties are sincerely trying to reach an agreement, they find themselves at an impasse. This is normally where the parties get frustrated and threaten to walk away from the whole deal.

I like to call this Broker Time! Time for the broker to earn their money. Let me share my motto with you:

RAIN, SLEET, OR SNOW, DON'T YOU WORRY,
YOU CAN COUNT ON JOE!

I know it's cheesy…I started that years ago with my restaurants inside office buildings. The restaurants were called "Joe's Place" and because rainy and snowy days were very good days, we made it a point to be open, no matter what. We were even open the day after hurricane Hugo…giving out ice before it melted and sandwiches to all that came in. Over the years it just stuck as a description of me personally. I don't mind the moniker as it does describe my loyalty and commitment to my friends and clients. And I guess I can be cheesy at times as well.

I like this motto because when the storm is about to sink the ship, the captain must remain calm! The way through the storm is to pass the shoals of contention and sail to the smaller areas of conflict in the negotiation. After you see the completed, larger picture of the deal, you will discover that perhaps the point of contention was not as big as you originally thought. This is a huge benefit of using a broker.

This challenging, emotional, and detailed process of buying a business is, ironically, what helps prepare you for owning a business. If you think this negotiating is hard, wait until you meet the employees, landlords, and suppliers. You can walk away from the deal if you have to, but you will not be able to walk away from the business once it's yours—and they know it!

I can remember the first time I tried to buy a piece of property. I was only 17 years old but, with the help of my mother and my dear friend, Leon Prenatt, the deal was completed.

Leon Prenatt was a real estate broker I met through Nick Evgenitakis, a boss of mine I worked for from the age of 14 through college. Nick taught me more about the restaurant business than any other person I know. Nick owned a restaurant in town and was doing some business with Leon, so I got to know Leon as a frequent customer of the restaurant. I can remember the day I deposited my check from work into my savings account, and the total equaled $2,000. "Wow!" I thought to myself, "I have saved $2,000!" That night I was bragging to Nick about my wealth and he suggested that I talk to Leon about investing it in a rental home.

I approached Leon the next time I saw him and said, "Mr. Prenatt, I have $2,000...can you help me spend it?" He laughed and said, "I can spend it in no time...I need a new car!" I said, "Well, that's not what I was thinking." He said, "Then ask me that question in a different way."

"I want to buy a home as a rental property," I said. "Can you help me?" He patted me on the back and said, "Let me see what I can do."

Three weeks went by and he never said anything to me about it. So one day I was looking in the paper for a home to buy and saw a house for sale: 411 Bradford, 2 bedroom, 1 bath, $12,000, block home, close to schools, for sale by Prenatt Realty, call today, could have you in fast!

Well, that sounded like a perfect deal for me, so I called Leon that minute and said, "Mr. Prenatt, you have a home for sale in the paper…why didn't you call me about it? I thought you were looking for a home for me, and this sounds great. Can I buy it?" I heard a laugh on the other end of the phone, and I said, "Did someone tell a joke…what is so funny?" He got very quiet, and there was a long silence. Then he said, "So Joe, you are serious, aren't you?"

"Absolutely," I said. "Do you think I can buy that home?" There was another long period of silence… "Joe, I think you may have found the one home that will work for you. Come on over to the office and we'll make this happen!"

From that phone conversation, Leon became one of my dearest friends, and he taught me more about real estate and negotiations than most people learn in two lifetimes!

Two months later, it was time to go to the closing of my first home. I recall walking into the attorney's office for the closing. Before entering the room, Leon looked at me and in a stern voice said, "Joe, you must ALWAYS BE WILLING TO WALK AWAY FROM A DEAL." I took that advice seriously and still rely on it today.

Through Leon's lessons, I have learned that treating all parties with respect during the negotiating process provides life-long, beneficial relationships. Evidence of this is that some years later, Leon personally financed my second restaurant, and we owned many properties together. Also, I am still using that first attorney and, to this day, I rely on Leon's son-in-law, Ken Green, for real estate advice and opportunities.

HERE ARE SOME OF MY THOUGHTS, GLEANED FROM MY YEARS OF EXPERIENCE WORKING WITH LEON PRENATT:

- **YOU MUST ALWAYS BE WILLING TO WALK AWAY FROM A DEAL AT ANY TIME.**

This does not mean the deal is done forever. Rather, it means not now, not today, not with these terms.

- **DO NOT BE AFRAID OF MAKING THE FIRST OFFER.**

With this approach, you get to set the starting point. The key to this strategy is to detail how the offer is to be structured. Terms. You want the buyer to see your thoughts on paper, but the offer has to sell itself, so make sure this is clear.

- **SOMETIMES YOU HAVE TO SAY, "THIS IS ALL I HAVE TO OFFER"**

I love this one because there is very little room for argument.

- **WIN\WIN IS A MYTH!**

The buyer must feel as though he/she came out on top or why write the check? The key in this, as I see it, is the seller must feel reasonably happy, but the winner must be (in their eyes) the buyer!

● KNOW YOUR LIMITS OF INTEREST AND CASH.

It's okay to let the seller know your thoughts because this may keep their expectations reasonable throughout the negotiating process.

● KNOW THE BUSINESS AND INDUSTRY TRENDS.

Most sellers get caught up in the operations and lose track of the industry itself and, therefore, do not see the negative trends. However, when informed of the negative trends, the seller will be more compelled to receive an offer from an informed buyer.

● "NEVER ... NEVER ... NEVER GIVE UP!" –*SIR WINSTON CHURCHILL*

Good negotiators do not give up. Perhaps you have to put the conversation on hold, but the negotiations are never over. Do not confuse this with my first point—"walking away simply means not today…not now." It does not mean never.

● IT'S NOT PERSONAL—IT'S JUST BUSINESS.

This is difficult, but make every effort to keep your emotions out of the equation. Your emotions will always cloud the outcome. This is where a good broker can help keep you in check.

> "It would be a mistake for me to lead you to believe that the negotiating process is always smooth and **painless.**"

"A dream paired with practical thinking and planning based on facts can produce results that you can't even imagine."

Chuck
Howell

aqa International

"If you want to run a charity, don't go into business. If you want to run a business, don't give it all away."

Phil
Fox

Fox Heating And Air

CHAPTER THIRTEEN

REMEMBER
who gave you
YOUR FIRST BREAK?

I have a plaque of this in my office just like the one I gave Leon Prenatt many years ago. Thank God I gave it to him before he died.

Someone saw something in you once. That's partly why you are where you are today. It could have been a thoughtful parent, a perceptive teacher, a demanding drill sergeant, an appreciative employer, or just a friend who dug down in his pocket and came up with a few bucks. Whoever it was had the kindness and the foresight to bet on your future. In the next 24 hours, take 10 minutes to write a grateful note to the person who helped you. You'll keep a wonderful friendship alive while giving something back to them. Then take another 10 minutes to give somebody else a break. Who knows? Someday you might get a nice letter. It could be one of the most gratifying messages you ever read.

71

"If you don't have a lot of belief in yourself, you will have a hard time leading your life to achieve your successes."

Michael
Nasr

Mr. Hero Sandwich Shop

CHAPTER FOURTEEN

MARKET
before you march

For several years now, I have been attempting to drill into my clients this simple directive: "Do not buy a small business unless you have a real, detailed plan of action that is substantially different than the seller's current operational model."

This can be summed up with three simple words: *Marketing ... Marketing ... Marketing.*

My experience suggests that there are many areas that need review and tweaking when you buy a small business but nothing jumps out as much as marketing.

CONSIDER THESE THOUGHTS:

• You must have a way to measure the effects of any marketing plan.

- There is not a better way to promote your business than networking. Every person you meet is a potential customer.

- Review the previous owner's marketing files and make sure your new plan has some old ideas reapplied.

- Professional marketing firms should not be your first step. These firms, while many times helpful, tend to be more costly and time consuming than most small businesses can afford.

- PR firms are of great benefit to a small business in branding both the owner and company in the community. Think of the PR firm as your personal agent, helping you through the maze of market opportunities.

- Go after the clients you want. You will never have the "dream client" unless you go get them!

- Know your customers! Find ways to learn who is coming to your establishment and why they are coming.

- Position your services or products correctly. Is your product or service vital to your client or is it merely an added expense for comfort? When you learn this, you must market your service or product accordingly.

- Take your time and hire right. Your employees are your most valuable form of marketing. You will do well to have an advisory group around you that can help you with all new hires.

- Pick up the phone and call the clients and customers you want—often!

BE READY FOR THE NEW BUSINESS. IT'S COMING!

CHAPTER FIFTEEN

SURVEYS

One of my favorite tools in gathering information about a business is to create a few surveys and ask the owner to mail or hand them out. The questions should not relay, in any way, that the business is for sale. They should look like the owner simply wants to improve customer relations.

Try to keep the surveys short and to the point—no more than seven questions. The purpose for these surveys is to see if your assumptions about the business you are evaluating are, in fact, correct. This is not something you can ask of a seller until they are sure you are sincere in your interest to buy. You may have to sell them on the idea that the information gained will be helpful to their business. Meanwhile, this is invaluable information if you do indeed buy the operation.

"Dedicate yourself to your goals."

Bob
Church

Magazine Development Corp.

CHAPTER SIXTEEN

LANDLORDS
and property owners

Ownership of the building for your business is always my first choice but, if this is not possible, make sure the relationship with the landlord (property management company) is not adversarial.

Take your time with the lease negotiations. Also make sure you get tenant mix clauses and minimum gross sale language. Try to get as much of your rent in the form of percentage rent. This form of rent is the fairest relationship for both parties. Also, it is important that you attempt to get a sizable amount of tenant up-fit allowance, which is a shared expense from the landlord and you on the actual up-fit cost of your new space which will, in time, benefit both parties.

Up-fit costs are reimbursements from landlords for work needed to get your new space ready for your operation. Most landlords will provide some money as an incentive to move into their space. I have seen this amount in a range from $5 - $25 per square foot.

Here is a list of occupancy cost averages. Remember, these are just rules of thumb; they are not set in stone. (This information was taken in part from the Business Reference Guide written and compiled by Tom West. Tom and his son, Ron, are some of my favorite people in the brokerage business.) Tom has helped many people over the years for little more than a "thanks." Tom and his company have written many books on this subject, so please visit his website at www.bbpinc.com.

RENT AS A [%] OF SALES:

Advertising agency – 2% to 3%
Apparel – 5% to 6%
Art Gallery – 2% to 3%
Auto Body Shop – 5% to 10%
Auto: new- 10% to 11% / used – 10% to 12%
Bagel Shops – 16% to 20%
Bakeries – 15% to 18%
Bars: adult – 7% to 10% / night clubs – 12% to 15%
Beauty salons – 9% to 10%
Bed & Breakfast – 9% to 10%
Bicycle shop – 6% to 7.5%
Bowling centers – 8% to 10%
Call centers – 3% to 4%

Camera shops – 2% to 3%

Camp grounds – 2.5% to 3.7%

Car washes (full) – 12% 14%

Carpet cleaning – 2.5% to 3.1%

Catering – 4% to 5%

Chiropractic practice – 6% to 7.5%

Clothing stores – 6% to 10%

Coffee shops – 8% to 12%

Coin laundry – 14% to 25%

Construction: site prep. – 8% to 10% / General – 5% to 10%

Convenient store /with gas – 7% to 8%

Day care – 15% to 20%

Dental practices – 6% to 7%

Direct mail (advertising) – 4.5% to 5.5%

Distribution: industrial – 1.5% to 2.5% / Medical – 2% to 3%

Dog grooming – 1% to 2%

Dog kennel – 7% to 10%

Dollar store – 4.5% to 5.5%

Donut shop – 8% to 11%

E-commerce – 4% to 5%

Fitness centers – 11% to 12.5%

Flower shop – 6% to 7.5%

Food services (contractors) – 7% to 10%

Franchise food service – 7% to 10%

Funeral homes – 4.5% to 5%

Furniture store – 4% to 5%

Garden centers – 2% to 3%

Gift shops – 5.5% to 7%

Golf courses – 4% to 5%

Grocery stores: small – 3% to 5%

Large – 2% to 3.5%

Hardware stores – 5% to 8%

Home health care – 4% to 5%

Hotel & motel – 65% to 70%

HVAC, contractors – 2% to 4%

Ice cream shops – 7% to 9%

Insurance agencies – 2% to 3%

Janitorial – 2.5% to 3%

Jewelry stores – 5% to 6%

Landscaping, lawn care – 2% to 5%

Law practices – 4% to 5%

Limousine service – 2% to 3%

Lumber yard – 3% to 5%

Manufacturing (general) – 3% to 5%

Marinas – 4% to 7%

Meat market – 8% to 10%

Medical practice – 3% to 4%

Moving & storage – 3% to 5%

Office staffing – 4% to 5%

Optical shops – 16% to 20%

Pizza shops – 6% to 8%

Print shops – 2% to 4%

Rental centers – 3% to 4%

Restaurants (full service) – 6% to 10%

Retail (general) – 15% to 18%

RV dealers – 1% to 2%

Shoe stores – 3% to 4%

Sporting goods store – 6% to 8%

Tanning salon – 6% to 8%

Taxi cab company – 3% to 4%

Tour operator – 11% to 15%

Towing company – 4% to 5%

Uniform rental – 2% to 3%

Vending – 1% to 2%

Wineries – 1% to 3%

"Take your time with the lease negotiations."

advisory BOARD

For years I have been telling small business owners to get themselves a formal advisory board. Very few ever do it. Most small business operators, however, have a group of people they bounce ideas off of already. While this is helpful, if you do not formalize the group, you only get minimal input. Once you get a formal group together, the respect and advice this group will give you is much greater.

My initial advisory board was formed almost without my knowledge. It certainly evolved in spite of my hardheadedness. Jim Cannon was the director and professor of the Hotel and Restaurant Management program at Central Piedmont Community College – where I graduated. As I was opening my first restaurant, Jim, who had become a dear friend to me (he even bought me my first sport coat so I could accompany him on a school trip), tried unsuccessfully to give me his wisdom and advice on things I needed to consider in opening this small business. I, however, thought I knew better, so I ignored nearly all his suggestions.

Within a few days of opening, Jim brought an entire class of students from the college to my establishment as a part of their class project. The assignment was to evaluate, critique, and offer suggestions for the betterment of my restaurant. I must confess that this proved to be a very embarrassing exercise for me because they clearly stated that most of what I was doing was in desperate need of improvement. Through all of this, I learned the life-long lesson of listening to the wisdom of those who have an interest in you and your business. Jim, even after doing all of this for me, offered and did bring the "who's who" of the local restaurant community by my place on a monthly basis to be a sounding board for me. This proved to be the beginning of my first advisory board. Thank you, Jim, for helping create my dream and also for teaching so many others that we can make dreams come alive, if we believe in ourselves and the power of God.

You must encourage and expect your advisory board to be completely open and honest with you. They must know that you need them to shoot straight with you, even if it is painful. This board must always have your best interests at heart and sometimes what they need to say to you will be difficult to hear. These folks will be your trusted allies in the venture. Sometimes in small business you will feel as if the entire world is against you, but these friends and confidants will prove to be your reminder that you are not alone in the fight. This advisory board will help you in numerous ways – especially in the hiring of professionals.

"I learned the life-long lesson of listening to the wisdom of those who have an interest in you and your business."

82

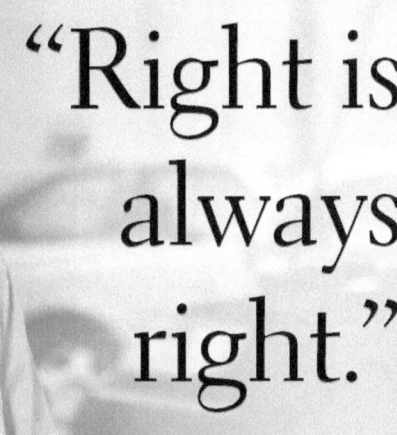

"Right is always right."

Sam
Hill

Hill And Sons
Automotive Services

Cast all your cares upon [Jesus]
for He cares for you.

- 1 Peter 5:7

scared, nervous, UNCOMFORTABLE ?

There is going to be a certain amount of trepidation as you move toward owning your own business. In many ways, the process of buying the business is what prepares you to own the business. Honestly, if you do not have some level of fear during the process, you are not ready to buy a business.

I can remember buying my first restaurant. It was a small, two-man operation, inside an office building. My dad helped me get it ready for the opening day. Dad has the strongest work ethic of any person I have ever known. His regular mantra was, "Come on boys keep up, you're burning daylight … let's knock this out … we've got work to do!"

We spent the entire weekend going at Dad's pace. When we were almost finished with the up-fit, Dad reached over and grabbed a candy bar from the rack. Realizing, of course, that since he would never stop for a break to eat, he saw this as just a little energy boost. As quickly as Dad took the candy bar, I stopped painting and immediately ran to the cash register and rang up the fifty-cent sale. My dad started to laugh uncontrollably. I asked, "What's so funny?" He said, as he was reaching in his pocket for the change, "I can't believe you are charging me, Son. I've just spent more than 53 hours helping you get this place ready!"

I was scared to death. Every penny I had was spent to get to this point. How could I possibly give something away? My dad, seeing the fear in my eyes, gently placed the two quarters on the counter. "Thanks, Dad," I said, "for being my first customer in business, and oh-yeah… thanks for the help!"

Fear is okay. It should help you focus, but do not let it stop you from your dreams. Look past the first thought of what could happen and see what you want to happen. Have a plan in place for the outcome you want.

This is why I tell clients to consider buying a business before they quit their job (and also to keep the other spouse working for a time). This allows the operation to show its true potential or lack thereof. If you have done your due-diligence, you will overcome your fears because you have a firm strategy and a plan of action.

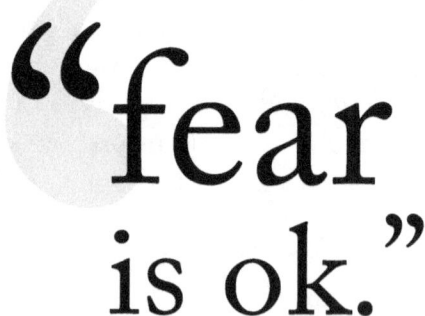

"fear is ok."

are you kidding?

M O R E   D E B T ?

I know, I know … everyone is telling you not to have debt … it's not healthy … it will slow you down … it will force you to make decisions you would normally not make. All that is true, but there is such a thing as good debt.

There is an easy way to tell if the debt you have is good or not. Before taking on any debt, ask yourself this question:

Does this asset I'm financing have potential to increase in value or produce income over time?

If the answer is yes then the debt is worth your consideration. If the answer is no, I would assert that you cannot afford what you are thinking about buying.

It's important for you to know that using credit wisely is a key factor in growth and, sometimes, future successes.

"I now open a little stationer's shop…(and) …
began now gradually to pay off the debt I was
under for the printing house."

- Benjamin Franklin,
Quoted from his autobiography

"Give your new business hard work and plenty of time before you ask it to repay you."

Penny
Hoover
12 Subway Franchises

franchise

OPPORTUNITIES

You would think that franchises for a guy like me would not be my first choice. But the truth is, I really like franchises for: First time buyers, older business owners, absentee owners, or part-time operators with full-time jobs. A franchise gives you a great baseline of where to go and how to get there and provides information about the business that otherwise would have taken you years to gather… if it is a good franchise. Let me reiterate: IF IT IS A GOOD FRANCHISE!

HERE ARE SOME RULES TO FOLLOW WHEN BUYING A FRANCHISE:

● <u>RULE 1: CALL AT LEAST 10 FRANCHISES IN THE SYSTEM PRESENTLY.</u>

- Are they making money?

I bet you hear something like "almost" or "we are just starting to break even." That is not making money. So the next question is, "So your answer is no…you are not making money right now, correct?"

● <u>RULE 2: TALK TO THE AREA DEVELOPER OR FRANCHISE DIRECTOR.</u>

- What do you do when a franchise returns your call and says, "I'm not making money; I need help"?

You will hear something like: "Because they are not following our program." So the next question is: "Can we call one of those franchises now, together? I would like to ask them a few questions with you on the call."

● <u>RULE 3: CALL AT LEAST THREE PEOPLE WHO HAVE LEFT THE FRANCHISOR'S SYSTEM AND ASK THESE QUESTIONS:</u>

- Why did you get out?
- What do you think of the area director?
- Did you get a fair price for the sale of the business?
- What is the best thing about the business and franchise?

Just let them talk and take notes as fast as you can!

● RULE 4: WHERE ARE THE LOCATIONS?

● What are the demographics of the top five franchise locations in the system? Call the owners of the five locations.

They better know this one because, next to the franchise owner\operator, location is the number one reason for success in franchising. If they say, "Well, one is beside a big school and another is by an office building ... and another is close to the highway ... blah, blah, blah, you need to insist on hard, clear, understandable, measurable demographics. Things like: traffic count, roof tops (homes in the area), owner occupied vs. rental, competitors plotted on a map, crime numbers, colleges with enrollment numbers, and any other questions you can think of. Create a worksheet and chart the five locations. Answer the question, "Why are they doing so well?" If at all feasible, go to the top stores and see what they are doing right.

● RULE 5: WHAT ARE THEIR WEAKNESSES?

● What is the biggest or most common complaint you hear from the customers?

This question will help you define where the franchise fits into the marketplace because you cannot be all things to everyone. Knowing where the competitors are having an advantage is very helpful in putting together your action plan.

● RULE 6: ONGOING TRAINING: IS IT HELPFUL?

● How often does the franchisor give you additional training? Is it helpful or just time consuming?

This question is so important because in a very short period of time you should know as much as the franchisor about your location and how to make it profitable. What you will need is the big picture and industry information that only a franchisor will have. If they do not provide this, then they are not a good franchisor in my opinion.

● <u>RULE 7: REGRETS?</u>

• What would you do differently if you were to start over?

Just let them talk and talk and talk. Find in the conversation the things that are personal and franchise-related, separate them, then evaluate the business—not the person.

● <u>RULE 8: DO YOU SEE THEM MUCH?</u>

• How often do they come to help or check the operation?

This one is so important but also so hard to talk about. The truth is, you would like to have someone come in to your business and help you with the things you are doing incorrectly. Or help in setting the direction for your marketing and operational plans. Sounds great! Well, I'll tell you, it's a humbling, frustrating process if it's not done with respect and from someone you trust. So here is the thing—you want to see them in your operation a lot, but treating you with respect. This goes back to rule 3. You need to trust the area director. And his/her advice should be welcomed. If that is the case, visits often are a good sign that the franchisor can be a real part of any solution when a problem comes up.

RULE 9: FAILURE?

- What is the failure rate for the last two years?

I promise you, if this rate is high in your area, you are in for a hard road to make a franchise succeed. It's probably best to move on. Even though it may be a fine franchise, to rebrand an operation is costly and time consuming.

RULE 10: DO YOU SEE YOURSELF BEHIND THE COUNTER?

- Do not buy a franchise to make money!

Buy it because you like the idea of working in that operation, and you have a vision of what can make it better. If you cannot see yourself behind the counter making ice cream and happy about it, do not buy an ice cream shop. I bet if you asked some of the present owners if they saw themselves behind the counter before they bought, and their answer was no, they would be the same folks that aren't doing well.

> "A franchise gives you a great base line of where to go and how to get there…that otherwise would have taken you years to gather."

"Provide your customer with more than they expect."

Chelsea
Bren

c Designs Photography & Print Design

franchise
RESALES

Over the years, I have bought and sold quite a few franchise operations. Utilizing various methods, I have gained experience in understanding what works best. Without question, the most successful approach has been purchasing an existing operation and making the changes that were recommended by the franchisor, as well as a few material alterations of my own.

My overarching rule about buying a business of any kind also applies to franchises: never buy a business without having an actual plan of action in place that provides for making substantive changes to the operation. Keeping things the same is not going to work for you. Remember, you will bear the additional cost of the purchase which is a burden the current owner does not have. In other words, you need to enter into this venture with the absolute goal of increasing and improving the business. Your plan cannot simply be generalizations about sales and customer service; it must include implementation of concrete ideas.

Before I closed on my third restaurant, I can remember my mother's dining room full of all the new stuff I was going to add to the business, and I wanted to get it all done in one weekend so that I would not have to close for remodel. It was a Monday through Friday operation so I knew I had the weekend—tv's, tables, chairs, marketing flyers, new menu, new equipment, giveaways etc. I was going to make sure that the customers knew this was not the same thing—just with different colors on the walls and new owners. I knew the more I could change, the more the customers would come in to see the changes. And my first week would be a great sales week. There have been times when my first week would pay for all the renovations in a small shop.

With all of this in mind, I have come up with a list of the benefits of buying an existing franchise (resale) as opposed to opening a new franchise:

- THE LOCATION HAS ALREADY BEEN TESTED

- INITIAL CASH FLOW

- THE PRESENT OWNERS CAN PROVIDE VALUABLE TRAINING THAT IS VERY LOCATION-SPECIFIC

- POTENTIAL SELLER-FINANCING OF THE PURCHASE

- IN SOME CASES, YOU CAN WORK UNDER THE PRESENT OWNER'S FRANCHISEE AGREEMENT

- VALUABLE CUSTOMER INFORMATION AND EXISTING MARKETING DETAILS

- HISTORY OF MARKETING PROGRAM SUCCESS OR FAILURE

- EXISTING LEASE AND FRAMEWORK FOR NEGOTIATIONS GOING FORWARD

- ABILITY TO ASSESS THE OPERATIONAL DETAILS OF THE BUSINESS AGAINST THE FRANCHISOR'S EXPECTATIONS

- ABILITY TO DETERMINE THE COST OF STARTING A NEW OPERATION BASED ON THE BALANCE SHEET OF THE CURRENT OPERATION AND MAKE COMPARISONS

- ABILITY TO EVALUATE THE EXISTING EMPLOYEES AND MAKE A JUDGMENT ABOUT THE POSSIBILITY OF IMPROVEMENT BASED ON THE JOB MARKET

- ACCESS TO INDUSTRY-WIDE AS WELL AS LOCAL MARKET TRENDS

With all these advantages, it is still important to do a full due-diligence on the franchisor and the franchisee. Both are very critical to your decision making. For example, if either of the entities does not meet my discerning standards or does not fit into my comfort zone, at that point during the process, I would be prepared to pull back and move on to the next deal.

Ultimately, you must realize that the true long-term relationship is with the franchisor. You must analyze the on-going operation and franchisee, but you must also look forward to the circumstances that lie ahead. That is the crucial mindset that leads to the future you seek.

Enjoy the search and remember to keep the process educational and fun as you will always benefit from your experience in business.

I will bless the Lord at all times:

His praise shall continually be in my mouth.

- Psalm 34:1

serious
BUSINESS!

Looking for a business opportunity is serious business in and of itself. After all, you will always expect people to take you seriously. I suggest you keep a file on each opportunity you consider and make a lot of notes. Bring your file with you to company tours and official meetings. The fact that you are serious will go a long way in the negotiations.

I have kept every deal I have ever looked at so that I can go back and compare the information to current opportunities and industry trends in the local area.

You will also want to put together a professional profile on yourself, including a financial statement. This will communicate to the potential seller your level of professionalism.

business due diligence
QUESTIONNAIRE

Here is a list of questions that will help you as you search for a small business opportunity. After getting answers to these questions, your knowledge of the business you're considering should be enough to get you comfortable with taking the next step in the process.

- BUSINESS NAME:

Legal & DBA

- FORM OF OWNERSHIP:

Individual, Partnership, # of partners, S Corp., or C Corp. Partners/Shareholders Names, % ownership or # of shares

- LOCATION:

Is there a lease? Tenant at will?
If owned and to be included in sale need copies of: Deed, Tax bill, and plot plan
Current lease has how many months remaining, how much per month, option to renew?

Current Lease expires
Does lease contain option to buy real estate?
Landlord's name
Is lease assignable? New lease available?
What is the rent per square foot next door? Across the street?
Parking: # cars, on street
Room for expansion?

- HISTORY:

Date founded, and/or date acquired
If acquired, the price paid
Brief overview of the company from its founding to the present

- THE BUSINESS:

Hours open
Square footage business occupies
Number of seats (if applicable)
Number of shifts
Special licenses required

- ASSETS:

Owner's estimate of values,
Orderly Liquidation Value (OLV) and average age
Furnishings, Fixtures and Equipment (FFE)
Leasehold improvements
Inventory
Vehicle(s) to be included
Patents, franchises, licenses etc.
Accounts receivable
Other

• STAFF:

Number of family members active in business: Full-time, Part-time
Number of non-family employees: Full-time, Part-time
Name of job, job description, hourly rate, hrs/wk, tenure (yrs)
Benefits provided and cost per employee
Employee employment contracts?
Copy of W-2s and 1099s for latest tax year
Labor pool for the company?

• OPERATIONS:

How much would you have to pay a manager in order to run this business "absentee"?
What percentage of supplies or inventory would be considered as dead or obsolete?
As a new Owner, how long would it take to be functional in this business?
From start up, how long to reach current level of profitability (months)?
How accurately can you predict revenues?
How much training is required to perform and understand this company's operations?
What is your Liability exposure level?
How important is the owner to the revenues of this business?
Over last three years, how have gross sales been trending
Explain how new business is obtained: (owners influence, walk in, direct mail, etc.)
What special license, degree or skills would a new owner need?

• OWNER'S BACKGROUND:

Owner's background prior to founding or acquisition: Education, Special skills or interests, Prior positions held

Owners duties and hours devoted to each per week:

Personnel Management   Sales/Marketing
Administration   Financial Mgmt
Production   Other
Customer service

- **SALES SEGMENTATION:**

How do you price your product/service?
Details of sales and target gross profit by segment
Recent price changes?

- **CUSTOMER BASE:**

Top 10 customers by volume for the past three years
Describe your typical customer
What other industries, businesses or customers could you serve?

- **COMPETITION:**

Major competitors
Name, Distance, Strengths/weaknesses
Number that have gone out of business in the last three years and why

- **GOVERNMENT AND REGULATIONS:**

Are there anticipated or actual changes in governmental regulations that will impact your business?
Are there environmental risks or hazardous materials used in or by this business?

- SALES AND MARKETING:

What efforts have you expended to grow the business?
What do you need to grow the business further? (Equipment, Staff, Financial)
Copies of independent party reports
Copies of OSHA reviews and reports
Copies of environmental audits or reports
Copies of sales, state, and federal tax reviews, audits or reports

- LIENS/DEBTS/ENCUMBRANCES:

Lender, Amount, Collateral

- MISCELLANEOUS:

Copies of pension/profit sharing plans
Declaration pages of all insurance policies
Pending litigation

- ADVISORS:

Attorney
Accountant
Insurance Agent
Consultants
Other

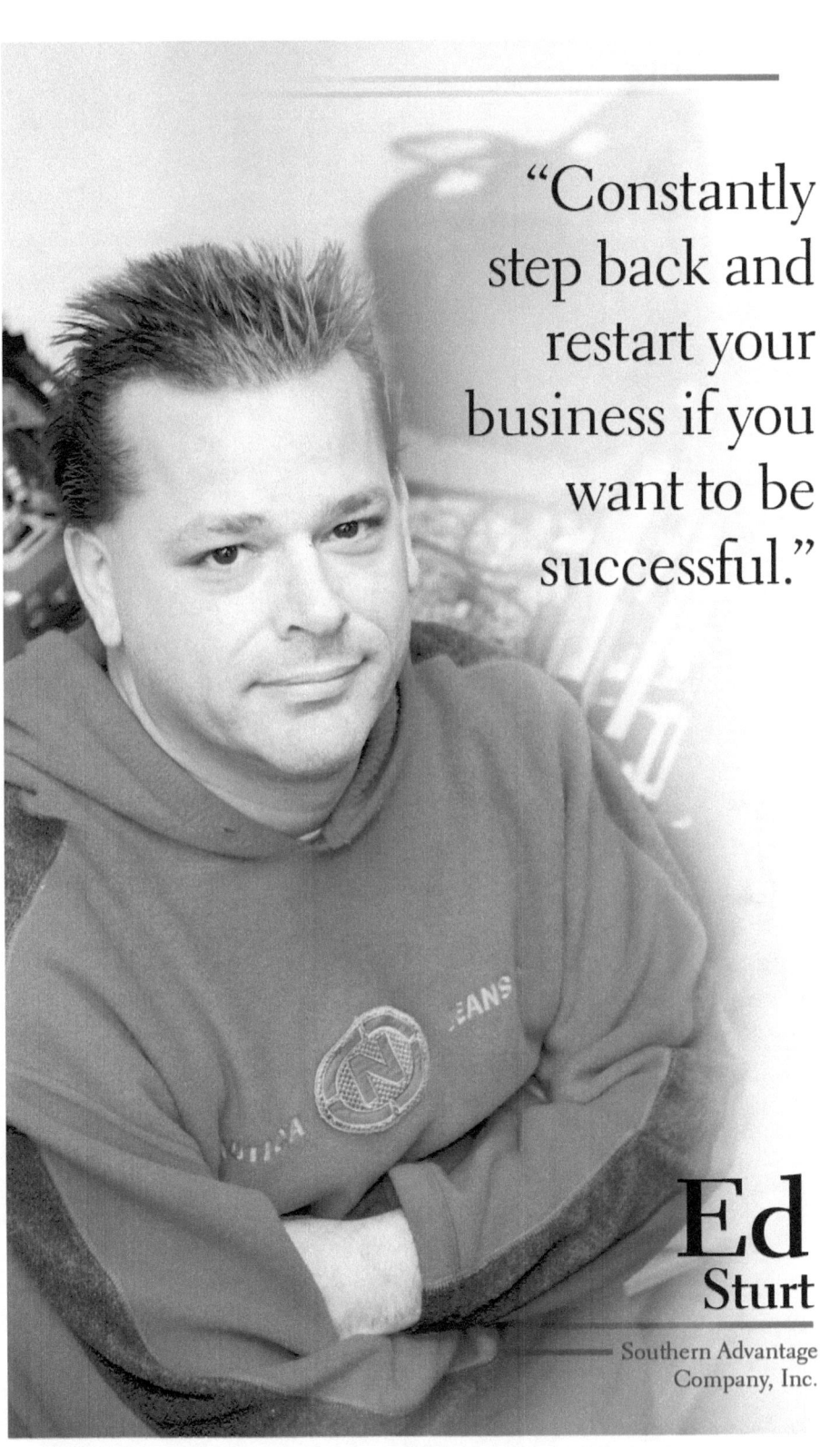

"Constantly step back and restart your business if you want to be successful."

Ed
Sturt

Southern Advantage
Company, Inc.

business
PROFILE

Here is a busines profile for your consideration.

Business Name:_____

The Business:
Form of Ownership: Individual _____ Partnership _____ # Partners _____
S Corp. _____ or C Corp._____ Business established in _____
Present Owner acquired in _____ If acquired amount paid $ _____
Down Payment $ _____

Describe this Business:
_____
_____
_____
_____
_____

Square Footage Business Occupies: _____ Number of Seats: _____

Special licenses required, vending contracts, franchise or license contracts:
_____
_____
_____
_____

Lease:
Presently Tenant at Will? Yes _____ No _____
Current lease has _____months remaining at $_____ per month with
option to renew for an additional period of_____years.
Current Lease expires on ___/___/___ Option to renew expires on ___/___/___
Rent under option to be $_____/ Month
Does lease contain option to buy Real Estate? _____

Landlord's Name _____

Telephone # _____

Address_____

Is Lease assignable? _____ New Lease available? _____

What is the rent per square foot next door? _____ Across the street? _____

Owner's estimate of Values, (Orderly Liquidation Value or OLV)

$ Value   Average Age

Furnishings, Fixtures and Equipment (FFE)   _____

Leasehold Improvement   _____

Inventory   _____

Vehicle(s) to be included in sale _____

Patents, Franchises, Licenses etc. (explain in notes) _____

Accounts Receivable   _____

Other   _____

Total OLV $ $_____

Staff:

Number of family members active in Business _____ List below:

Name	Job Description	Pay Rate	Hrs/Wk	# yrs

Number of non-family employees: Full-time_____ Part-time_____

Name	Job Description	Pay Rate	Hrs/Wk	# yrs

Operations:

Hours Open: _____

days open: _____

How much would you have to pay a manager in order to run this Business "absentee"? $_____

What percentage of supplies or inventory would be considered as dead or obsolete? _____

What percent of your FFE should be replaced yearly to maintain a good image and productivity? _____

As a new Owner, how long would it take to be functional in this Business? _____

From start up, how long to reach current level of profitability (months)? _____

How accurately can you predict Revenues (explain): _____
_____
_____
_____

How much training is required to perform and understand this company's operations: _____
_____
_____
_____

What is your Liability exposure level_____

How important is the Owner to the Revenues of this Business? _____
_____
_____

Over the last three years, how have Gross Sales been trending? _____
_____
_____

New business is obtained by: (Owner's influence, walk in, direct mail, etc.)
_____

What special license, degree or skills would a new owner need? _____
_____
_____
_____

How do you price your product or service? _____
_____
_____
_____

Present marketing strategy?_____
_____
_____

Most businesses can be segmented and profit margins identified by segments. Identify below.

Major Categories or Segments	Target Gross Profit	% of Volume
_____	_____	_____
_____	_____	_____

Customers:
How many Customers does the Business serve?_____
What number of Customers account for 25% of Volume? _____

Industry:
Considering social status, visual appeal, profits, etc. how desirable is this Business or Industry? _____

Have liability insurance rates gone up? _____ How much? _____

What is the trend for this Industry?_____

What is the status of local labor pools for this Business? _____

Does your industry have a "Trade Association?"? _____
If yes, are you a member? _____
Association(s): _____
_____
_____
_____

Overview:
What are the businesses strong pointsstrong points of the business? _____
_____
_____
_____

What are the opportunities? _____
_____
_____

How could the business be improved? _____
_____
_____

Competition:
How many Competitors in the marketing area?_____
How many have failed in the last two years ? _____
How many are new (within the last two years)? _____

Impending Changes:
Traffic flow, government regulations, zoning and competition, etc.? _____
If yes, how would the Business be affected positively and/or negatively?____
_____
_____
_____

Banking:

Have lenders loaned on the assets of the Business alone? _____

Which Bank(s) does the Business use and what is the relationship?

Bank	Service Utilized	Loan Officer	Phone

Outstanding Notes:

Assumable? Indicate with an X if No

Lender	Security	% Interest	Term	Current Payoff?

"You can achieve whatever you can visualize and believe. Be prepared to work 24-7 for 5 years and have enough capital to keep you going for 2-3 years without paying yourself."

James
Cannon

Retired from Central Piedmont Community College where he developed the nationally recognized Hospitality Education Program

planning on
CLOSING

H ere are a few things that you will need to consider when planning for your closing on the purchase of your new business.

Accounting program setup

Sales tax number

Government requirements

Business licenses

Phone/Utility account changes

Dumpster account changes

Supplier account changes

Payroll service

Security account
& password

Final inventory & initial purchases needed

Corporate attorney
(should be different from
personal attorney)

Corporate accountant

closing requirements
CHECKLIST

( ) **1.** Offer to Purchase and Amendments with separate sheet showing "final" deal.

( ) **2.** All Deposits (including down payment) in Escrow as Collected Funds.

( ) **3.** Contingencies Removed List - with check offs.

( ) **4.** Lease Assignment, New Lease or Letter of Intent signed by Lessor.

( ) 5. Commission Agreement.

( ) 6. Compliance Letters including those required by government, signed by both Buyer and Seller with checks.

( ) 7. Escrow Authorization signed by Buyer and Seller.

( ) 8. List of Creditors with addresses, zip codes and telephone numbers (if Bulk Transfer) unless waived by attorneys.

( ) 9. LEGIBLE Equipment List signed by Seller.

( ) 10. Covenant Not to Compete signed (if applicable).

( ) 11. Agreement to Train signed (if applicable).

( ) 12. Bank Commitment Letter (if Bank Loan).

( ) 13. Articles of Incorporation, Corporate Resolution to Sell and Corporate Seal for closing (if Seller is Corporation).

( ) 14. Seller's existing Deed (if Real Estate Transaction).

( ) **15.** Motor Vehicle Title(s).

( ) **16.** Insurance on Building, Assets, Health, etc. checked and entered on Proration Schedule.

( ) **17.** Workman's Comp and other "prepaids"

( ) **18.** Lien search

( ) **19.** UCC Searches, all contracts, security agreements, etc. done by Attorneys.

( ) **20.** Asset allocation signed by both parties.

( ) **21.** COMPLETE, CORRECT, LEGIBLE, list of all names, addresses, zip codes and telephone numbers of each person whose name will appear on a document, ie: Buyers, Sellers, Lessors, (and address where rent will be sent).

( ) **22.** Purchase price allocation with Promissory note

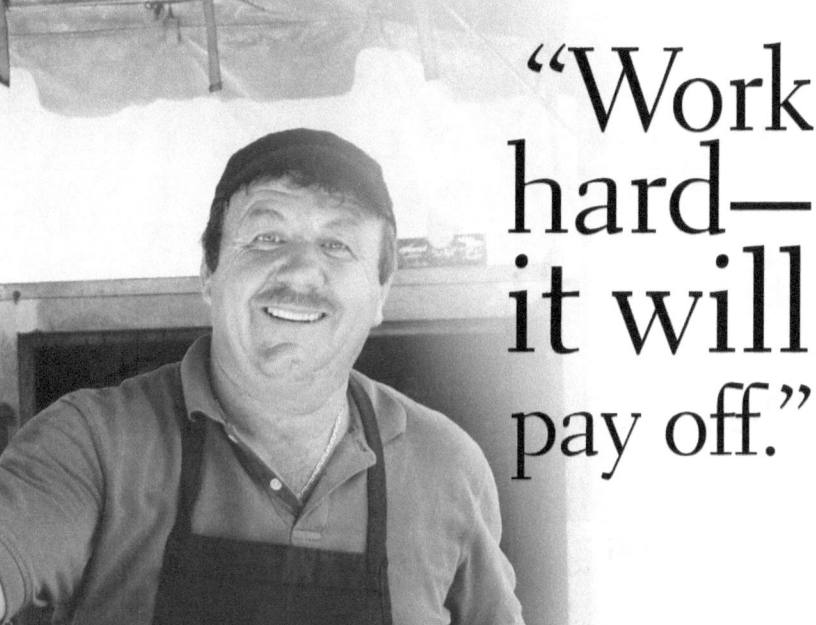

"Work hard— it will pay off."

Kostas "Gus"
Holevas

Gus' Tree Service/Event Catering

There is a way that seems right unto man
but the end thereof is destruction.

- Proverbs 14:12

manage your
TIME

To get right to the point, if you are not in control of your time and manage it well, your business will run your life, and the search for a business will take much longer as well.

To help prevent this, I will tell you one of my favorite statements:

"I had a lot of friends before I owned my own business." The statement is an exaggeration but the point is that you must learn and embrace the word "NO." You will find, as I did, that some of the best deals I made were the ones I did not do. I have another statement that drives my friends crazy: "My phone is for my convenience," not so you can talk to me any time you want. It sounds cold-hearted but you have to get control of the things that are controllable because in small business so many things are not. You must be prepared to act and react quickly. You cannot do that if personal relationships are demanding too much time at the same time attention is needed to run the business. The business will not wait. A true friend will.

Saying "No" goes for buying a business as well as running one. There is a time to stop the due-diligence and simply walk away. Spend your time on evaluating a different opportunity. Wasting time on a business in an industry that you just do not feel comfortable with is not education; it is valuable time wasted. You are never going to know everything about every industry, but you should know as much as you can about the industry you are interested in. And, be sure to be enthusiastic!

"If you are not in control of your time…your business will run your life."

"My early days were spent trying to wear all the different hats in running my business. It took me awhile to realize that my focus needed to be on the top line. Sales solve ALL problems."

Dave Taylor

Your Office @ Ballantyne

"Find the best possible people, invest in them, and empower them to become excellent."

Roy
Mason

Global Evangelism Ministries

knowing when
TO SELL

The first thing to guard against is the type of rash, emotion-driven judgment that leads to regret and resentment after you have pulled the rug out from under yourself. Selling your business, which for many represents a life's work or a lifetime of savings, should not be considered lightly or in haste.

There may come a time, however, when dissatisfaction creeps into the picture. Daily operations may become too much like a chore, or outside interests may pull your focus away from your business. These may be indications that it is time to consider a change of some kind. The impetus for looking to other opportunities can be as simple as rekindling the initial excitement you had when you first started your business. It is worthwhile to take the time to truly remember your feelings of that first love. It is a mental exercise that I encourage and recommend to anyone who is contemplating change. This type of sorting out sometimes requires a long vacation, but do not confuse "needing a break" with "needing a total change."

As a small business owner, you become aware of what makes you successful in your field—the passion and intimate knowledge of the industry in which you are engaged. All the extra hours you spent thinking of a new and better way to accomplish things did not seem like

"Holding on too long is a common mistake."

work, per se, but felt good and honorable and maybe even defined your life for a time. But if you find the energy and drive disappearing from your efforts, and the joy you once had of starting every day with purpose and exhilaration becomes drudgery and a burden, it is time to take particular notice. When this happens, you run the risk of watching your operation start to decline. This can happen at such an imperceptible pace that one day you realize your business has fallen from the successful height to which you have built it. New competitors, customer loss and falling sales are the result of a lack of focus. Eventually, the years spent taking from your business instead of working in your business takes its toll.

Before finding yourself in this situation or worse, it might be beneficial to you, your family, and the business, to think about moving on. My experience has been that most owners start the process of selling their operation years after the value of their business has declined. Holding on too long is a common mistake. At the least, have a plan so that when you are ready for transition, valuable time will be saved. This directly translates into more money and value to the operation.

This process is called exit planning. Research in this area will be required, with the help of professionals, as there are tax and legal considerations. Also, the strategy directed at the timing of your actions plays an important role as well. Think of your exit plan just as you would a business plan, that all-important design you started with that got your business off the ground. The difference, of course, is your exit plan is part of your business plan for the future endeavors of your life. This time, it will involve an asset sale with a reinvestment element that smoothes the transition toward the next exciting chapter of your life.

Again, take your time thinking of what your future will look like. This can bring back the fun and the anticipation you relished in the beginning. If you sell your business at the right time and in the right manner, you will have the cash and a sound plan to make decisions going forward. Have fun!

ENJOY THE SEARCH
for a new beginning.

129

www.ingramcontent.com/pod-product-compliance
Lightning Source LLC
Chambersburg PA
CBHW022005170526
45157CB00003B/1152